Telling Isn't Tattling

Kathryn M. Hammerseng
Illustrated by Dave Garbot

Parenting Press, Inc.
Seattle, Washington

A Note for Grown-ups

Children often tattle when they are learning rules. If a child tattles you have several options—

- You can ignore the comment or say, "Ummm."
- You can ask, "What can you do to solve the problem yourself?" or, "Was that tattling or telling?"
- You can offer your child two ways to get attention without tattling. For example, say gently, "That was tattling. If you want my attention, you can ask for a hug or offer to help me."
- You can help the child decide what to do. For example, you can ask,

> "What have you already tried?"
> "What else can you do?"
> "What will you try first?"

Copyright © 1995 by Kathryn M. Hammerseng
Cover and text illustrations © 1995 by Parenting Press, Inc.

Manufactured in the United States of America
First edition,

Library of Congress Cataloging-in-Publication Data

Hammerseng, Kathryn M., 1962.
  Telling isn't tattling / Kathryn M. Hammerseng,
      p.   cm.
  Summary: Distinguishes between telling and tattling and explains the motivations behind tattling.
  ISBN 1-884734-07-3 (lib. bdg.) – ISBN 1-884734-06-5 (pbk.)
  1. Social interaction–Juvenile literature. 2. Interpersonal relations–Juvenile literature. 3. Talebearing–Juvenile literature. 4. Social skills in children. 5. Social skills in children–Study and teaching, [1. Talebearing.] I. Title.
HO784.S56H36   1995
303.3'2–dc20   95-12125
                                                CIP

Telling Isn't Tattling

Telling isn't tattling. However, many children and adults have trouble knowing the difference. This book will help you tell the difference.

Children *tattle* when they want to—
- get someone in trouble,
- look good in someone else's eyes,
- get attention,
- have an adult solve their problem.

Children are *telling* when they—
- want protection for themselves or someone else,
- want protection for their own or someone else's property,
- are scared,
- are in danger.

Read each story and decide whether the child is telling or tattling. When you have decided what you think, ask yourself why you think that. You may want to refer to the rules above for help. Then read what the author thinks.

Reading this book together will help families tell the difference between telling and tattling.

Tony and Mike are outside playing. They both want to ride the bike. Tony runs fast and gets it first.

"Stupid!" yells Mike.

"Am not!" answers Tony, and he bursts into tears.

"Baby! Baby! Tony is a crybaby!" teases Mike.

"I'm not a baby, and don't call me names!" says Tony.

"Baby, baby, baby," chants Mike. Tony stops listening to Mike. After a while, Mike gets tired of teasing Tony and starts to play on the swing.

Tony still feels mad at Mike, so he goes inside to tell his mother.

Is Tony telling or tattling?

Tony is tattling. He is trying to get Mike in trouble. He already solved his problem. Since Mike stopped calling him names, Tony doesn't need his mother's help.

What else can Tony do?

▶ Tony can ride around his driveway really fast on his bike until his anger is gone.

▶ Tony can think about something that makes him feel good.

▶ Tony can tell his teddy bear how he feels.

▶ Add your ideas.

What would you try first?

SNiff

Patrick and Cheryl are sitting at the kitchen table having a snack. Cheryl accidently knocks her glass of juice off the table and it breaks.

"Oh, oh! Broken glass can cut us," says Patrick. "We should go get Dad to help us clean it up right away."

"No. I'm big enough," says Cheryl. "I'll do it."

Patrick goes to tell Dad anyway.

Is Patrick telling or tattling?

Patrick is telling. The broken glass is dangerous. He and Cheryl need their dad's help. He is helping Cheryl even though she doesn't want him to tell Dad. Patrick can also help Cheryl by explaining to Dad that she knocked the glass off accidently.

What else can Patrick and Cheryl do to make things safe?

▶ Patrick and Cheryl can leave the kitchen and close the door until a grown-up comes to help clean up.

▶ They can put their shoes on so their feet won't get cut.

▶ They can make a barrier of chairs around the broken glass.

▶ Add your ideas.

What would you try first?

Stephen doesn't like it when his Uncle Pete tickles him. Even when he yells at him to stop and tells him his stomach hurts, Uncle Pete won't quit.

"Stop tickling me, Uncle Pete. You're hurting me," cries Stephen.

"Oh, come on. This is fun," laughs Uncle Pete.

Stephen isn't having fun and he tells his dad.

Is Stephen telling or tattling?

Stephen is telling. He needs protection. He didn't like the way Uncle Pete was touching him. He asked him to stop, but he didn't. He knows his dad will speak to Uncle Pete and tell him to quit.

Whenever anyone touches you, even if they are playing, and it doesn't feel good or right, tell them to stop and tell a grown-up whom you trust.

What else can Stephen do?

▶ Stephen can stay near his mom or dad when Uncle Pete is visiting.

▶ Stephen can go to his room and close the door.

▶ Stephen can tell his grandparent or another adult friend whom he trusts.

▶ Add your ideas.

What would you try first?

Felicia and Emily had a lot of fun playing a game, but are tired of it now.

"You put the game away," says Emily to Felicia.

"Okay," she says cheerfully, as she puts the game on the closet floor.

Emily knows that games go on the shelf, too high for Felicia to reach, but she doesn't say anything.

Dad comes into the room. "Good job, Felicia. You picked up the game."

Emily feels hurt. No one notices when she puts things away.

"Look, Dad. Felicia put the game on the floor," Emily whines.

Is Emily telling or tattling?

Emily is tattling. She hopes that Felicia will get in trouble with Dad. Telling on someone to make them look bad so you will look good is tattling. If people don't notice the good things you do, it's okay to tell them.

What else can Emily do?

▶ Emily can help her little sister put the game away in the right place.

▶ Emily can show her dad something she has done well.

▶ Emily can ask her mom or dad to tell her when she has done things well, too.

▶ Add your ideas.

What would you try first?

Things aren't too nice at Jessica's house. Her dad gets mad a lot. When he gets real mad, he hits Jessica's mother.

"Mom, it scares me when Dad hits you. Tell him to stop, please," says Jessica.

"Well, it doesn't hurt very much. Don't tell anyone. This is our secret," Mom says.

But Jessica is scared. She tells a teacher whom she trusts.

Is Jessica telling or tattling?

Jessica is telling. Someone is being hurt and she is scared. Even though her mother asked her not to tell, she is helping her mother to be safe. Anytime you or someone you know is being hurt, you should tell a grown-up whom you trust and get help right away.

What else can Jessica do?

▶ Jessica can tell her grandma about what is happening.

▶ Jessica can tell a friend's mother whom she trusts.

▶ Jessica can call the police by dialing 911 if it happens again.

▶ Add your ideas.

What would you try first?

Nick and Amy are playing outside in Nick's playhouse.

"If you pull your pants down, I'll pull mine down," says Nick.

"No, I don't want to," says Amy.

Nick pulls his pants down anyway and starts to pull Amy's down, too.

This feels icky to Amy, so she goes to tell Nick's mom about it.

"Boys are like that sometimes," says Nick's mom. "Go on back out and play."

Amy goes home and tells her mother about it.

Is Amy telling or tattling?

Amy is telling. Amy needs protection. Nick wanted to do something that doesn't feel good to her. His mother wouldn't listen to her. Amy did the right thing by finding another grown-up to tell. If one grown-up won't listen, you should find another one who will.

What else can Amy do?

► Amy can call her dad at work.

► Amy can tell her older brother or sister.

► Amy can tell a neighbor whom she trusts.

► Add your ideas.

What would you try first?

Cory's mom and dad are going out and leaving Cory with Julie, his baby sitter. Cory likes her a lot and has fun playing games with her. But he misses his mom and dad. He wishes they would take him along, or stay home with him.

"Julie, you're not supposed to talk on the phone," says Cory.

"It'll just take a minute. I need to get a homework assignment," says Julie.

When Dad and Mom get home, Cory tells them, "Julie called her friend while you were gone!"

Is Cory telling or tattling?

Cory is tattling. He is trying to get Julie in trouble so she can't babysit anymore. He wants his parents to stay at home with him. Cory needs to think of other ways to get the attention he wants.

What else can Cory do?

▶ Cory can ask his parents to take him somewhere with them.

▶ Cory can ask his mom or dad to call him while they are out.

▶ Cory can play a tape of his dad reading their favorite story.

▶ Add your ideas.

What would you try first?

Molly frowns as she sees her dad's friend, John. He comes over often and says things she doesn't like.

When Dad goes into the kitchen to fix dinner, John says to her, "We can be extra special friends if I could touch you all over."

Molly is afraid John will get mad at her if she says no. But she doesn't want to let him touch her. She is embarrassed to tell her dad, so she talks to her grandma.

Is Molly telling or tattling?

Molly is telling. She is scared and needs protection. John wants to do something that doesn't feel good to her. She needs help from a grown-up whom she trusts right away.

If someone wants to touch you in a way you don't like, or asks you to touch them, say no and get help from a grown-up whom you trust.

What else can Molly do?

▶ Molly can ask her best friend's mother to talk to her dad.

▶ Molly can tell her preschool teacher.

▶ Molly can tell her older brother or sister.

▶ Add your ideas.

What would you try first?

20

Tyler and Greg are at the beach. Tyler has built a large sand castle and is driving his truck around it.

Greg is mad. His sand castle keeps falling down. He stomps on Tyler's sand castle.

"Look, Tyler! Your castle fell down, too," he shouts.

"Hey, stop it!" Tyler protests.

Greg begins to stomp on Tyler's truck.

"Don't break my truck!" Tyler yells, while Greg kicks at it.

Tyler runs to tell Aunt Peg.

Is Tyler telling or tattling?

Tyler is telling. He tried to solve his problem himself. When someone tries to break something and won't stop, you need to ask a grown-up for help.

What else can Tyler do?

▶ Tyler can take his truck away and put it beside Aunt Peg.

▶ Tyler can offer to help Greg build his sand castle so it won't fall down.

▶ Tyler can say, "Let's look for seashells."

▶ Add your ideas.

What would you try first?

Lupita feels sad. She is having a hard time at day care. She's crying because her kitty was run over by a car.

"Stop being a crybaby," says one of the teachers. "I'll have to give you a time-out if you keep it up."

Lupita tells her mother what the teacher said as they walk home.

"She's really mean. Will you tell her not to be mean to me?" she asks her mom.

Is Lupita telling or tattling?

Lupita is telling. Lupita doesn't feel comfortable or safe. Someone who is supposed to be taking care of her is not doing a very good job. She is doing the right thing by telling her mother.

Whenever you feel unsafe or uncomfortable about the people taking care of you, you should tell a grown-up whom you trust.

What else can Lupita do?

▶ Lupita can tell her teacher, "I feel sad because my kitty was run over by a car."

▶ Lupita can ask another teacher, "Will you give me a hug?"

▶ Lupita can draw a picture of how she feels and talk about it with her dad.

▶ Add your ideas.

What would you try first?

Naomi and Taro are in the field flying a kite on a warm, windy day.

"I'll hold the string and you watch," says Taro.

Naomi wants a turn holding the string, too.

After a few minutes of waiting for Taro to share, she goes to tell their dad.

She hopes he'll make Taro give her a turn holding the kite string.

Is Naomi telling or tattling?

Naomi is tattling. She didn't try to solve her problem herself. Taro doesn't know she wants a turn because she didn't tell him.

Telling on someone to get them to do what you want is tattling. If you want someone to do something, ask or tell them what it is. They might do it, or they might not.

What else can Naomi do?

▶ Naomi can ask Taro, "May I have a turn now?"

▶ Naomi can offer to trade a turn with her favorite toy for a turn with the kite.

▶ Naomi can ask her dad for another kite.

▶ Add your ideas.

What would you try first?

Chanda and Jamie are playing outside. A man drives slowly up to the curb and calls out to them.

"Come get in my car and I'll take you both for ice cream cones," he says.

The two children run right into the house without stopping to answer.

They tell Jamie's mom about the man in the car.

Are Chanda and Jamie telling or tattling?

The children are telling. They are in danger. Jamie's mom will know what to do to keep them safe. If you are ever in danger, go quickly to someone whom you trust who will keep you safe. Tell them exactly what is happening.

Never get into anyone's car without asking a grown-up whom you trust if it is okay. Even if the driver is someone you know, whoever is looking after you needs to know where you are all the time.

What else can Chanda and Jamie do?

▶ Chanda and Jamie can move far away from the car.

▶ They can yell as loudly as possible so that someone will hear who can help them.

▶ Chanda and Jamie can ask a neighbor for help, if their homes aren't nearby.

▶ Add your ideas.

What would you try first?

Olivia, Michelle, and Rosa are out on the school playground. Olivia and Michelle are playing on the jungle gym.

Rosa runs up and jumps onto the high rung, bumping into Olivia.

"Hey! Watch what you're doing," yells Olivia. "I was here first."

Michelle says, "Yeah, we were here first. Go play somewhere else."

Rosa runs over to the playground monitor and tells her, "Michelle and Olivia won't let me play on the jungle gym."

Is Rosa telling or tattling?

Rosa is tattling. She didn't try to solve her problem herself.

What else can Rosa do?

▶ Rosa can ask Michelle and Olivia if she can play with them.

▶ Rosa can ask for a turn on the jungle gym.

▶ Rosa can play with someone or something else.

▶ Add your ideas.

What would you try first?

Who Can Help You?

Make a list of the people you feel comfortable and safe with. You can write their names or draw pictures of them. Write their telephone numbers beside their names or pictures.

	Name _____
	Day Telephone _____
	Eve. Telephone _____

	Name _____
	Day Telephone _____
	Eve. Telephone _____

	Name _____
	Day Telephone _____
	Eve. Telephone _____

	Name _____
	Day Telephone _____
	Eve. Telephone _____

If you need help and you don't know any grown-up around you, choose anyone who feels safe to you. This might be a grown-up with children or someone in a store or office.

"What Would You Do If . . . ?"

Telling Isn't Tattling helps children learn when to tell an adult they need help. It also helps adults learn when to pay attention to kids' requests for help.

You can continue exploring the differences between telling and tattling. Make up your own stories by playing "What would you do if . . . ?"

The rules for telling the difference are:
Children *tattle* when they want to—

> ► get someone in trouble,
> ► look good in someone else's eyes,
> ► get attention,
> ► have an adult solve their problem.

Children are *telling* when they—

> ► want protection for themselves or someone else,
> ► want protection for their own or someone else's property,
> ► are scared,
> ► are in danger.

Have fun exploring together!

Order these books
for ideas on safety for children

It's MY Body
Teaches young children how to resist uncomfortable touch.

by Lory Freeman Illustrated by Carol Deach

$5.95 paper, $15.95 library, 32 pages. Also in Spanish

The Trouble with Secrets
Helps children distinguish between hurtful secrets and
good surprises.

by Karen Johnson Illustrated by Linda Johnson Forsse

$5.95 paper, $15.95 library, 32 page

Telling Isn't Tattling
Helps children distinguish the difference between
telling and tattling.

by Kathryn M. Hammerseng Illustrated by Dave Garb

$5.95 paper, $16.95 library, 32 pa

Ask for these books at your favorite bookstore
or call Parenting Press, Inc. at **1-800-992-6657.**
VISA and MasterCard accepted.
Complete book catalogue available on request.

Prices subject to change without notice.

**Parenting Press, Inc.
Dept. 504, P.O. Box 75267
Seattle, WA 98125**

SEP 29 2003